# Burns Braille Guide

## A Quick Reference to Unified English Braille

### Second Edition

*Mary F. Burns*

AFB **PRESS**

American Foundation for the Blind

Printed in the United States of America

Library of Congress Cataloging-in-Publication Data

Burns, Mary F., 1962- author.
　Burns braille guide : a quick reference to Unified English Braille / Mary F. Burns. — Second edition.
　　　pages cm
　ISBN 978-0-89128-717-9 (pbk. : alk. paper) — ISBN 978-0-89128-729-2 (online subscription) — ISBN 978-0-89128-730-8 (epub) — ISBN 978-0-89128-731-5 (mobi)　1. Braille—Handbooks, manuals, etc.　I. Title.
　HV1672.B867 2015
　411—dc23
　　　　　　　2015027711

The American Foundation for the Blind removes barriers, creates solutions, and expands possibilities so people with vision loss can achieve their full potential.

It is the policy of the American Foundation for the Blind to use in the first printing of its books acid-free paper that meets the ANSI Z39.48 Standard. The infinity symbol that appears above indicates that the paper in this printing meets that standard.

# Contents

# Acknowledgments

I'd like to thank Diane Finn, Coordinator of Vision Programs, Northern Illinois Association, for her support and her input. Diane, I'm so glad I came to work for you, oh so long ago.

I'd also like to thank Dr. Frances Mary D'Andrea, Educational Consultant in Visual Impairments and Chair of Braille Authority of North America (BANA), my go-to person for explaining some of the rules to me. Okay, a *lot* of the rules. Really. A lot. Thank you, Dr. D'Andrea!

# Introduction

When I first heard we were changing the braille code from EBAE (English Braille, American Edition) to UEB (Unified English Braille), I was as excited as everyone else. I'd been using the EBAE code for 30 years, and now I had the opportunity to learn a new one. Then it struck me that the original edition of this book would soon become obsolete.

The changes in the code from EBAE to UEB are both obvious and subtle. Some contractions are no longer used, some have undergone modifications, and others have experienced some rule changes. Since it will be some years before we stop seeing the EBAE code in braille publications, for this edition of the book I chose to include both the UEB and the EBAE code in the Braille to Print section. The EBAE contractions, signs, and additional elements are listed with an "EBAE code" notation.

In the General Rules and Terminology section, I've listed much of the terminology that we find in the UEB code. Also, I've given a few general rules for braille transcribing. However, it is difficult to list rules in a generalized format because braille transcribing loves exceptions. For example, "Always follow the print, *except* for ornamentation. Do not transcribe ornamentation *except* when it is a facsimile."

In the Punctuation, Symbols, and Indicators section there is a column indicating where to locate the specific rules. These will be found in the second edition of *The Rules of Unified English Braille*, published by the International Council on English Braille (ICEB; Simpson, 2013).

Shortform words are no longer "rule-based" but are now "list-based." The list of approved shortform words appears in the appendix to this edition with permission from ICEB. The list of General

Rules and Terminology is also based on *The Rules of Unified English Braille*.

This book is set up to be a reference guide similar to those French-to-English, English-to-French pocket language dictionaries. However, in this case, it is braille-to-print, print-to-braille. It is important to remember that this book is not to be used as an instruction manual. The *Burns Braille Guide* is a quick reference guide for those who already know contracted or grade 2 braille, such as teachers of students with visual impairments, vision rehabilitation therapists, braille transcribers, braille readers, paraprofessionals, and parents. Those who know uncontracted or grade 1 braille will also find it helpful for looking up grade 1 symbols.

I hope readers find this book as useful as I expect to myself.

## REFERENCE

Simpson, C. (Ed.). (2013). *The Rules of Unified English Braille* (2nd ed.). Lindisfarne, Australia: Round Table on Information Access for People with Print Disabilities Inc. and International Council on English Braille. Retrieved from http://www.iceb.org/ueb.html

# The Unified English Braille Alphabet

Including Numbers and Common Punctuation and Composition Signs

| a | b | c | d | e | f | g | h | i | j |
|---|---|---|---|---|---|---|---|---|---|

| k | l | m | n | o | p | q | r | s | t |
|---|---|---|---|---|---|---|---|---|---|

| u | v | w | x | y | z | capital letter | numeric indicator | , | . |
|---|---|---|---|---|---|---|---|---|---|

| 1 | 2 | 3 | 4 | 5 | 6 | 7 | 8 | 9 | 0 |
|---|---|---|---|---|---|---|---|---|---|

| ; | : | - | ' | ! | ( | ) | ? | " | " |
|---|---|---|---|---|---|---|---|---|---|

# 1

# General Rules and Terminology

The following is a list of select UEB rules and terminology. This is not a complete list, but rather, for the purposes of this book, a list of the most commonly used rules and terminology. For a complete list, please refer to the International Council on English Braille *Rules of Unified English Braille* (Simpson, 2013).

## GENERAL RULES ABOUT BRAILLE TRANSCRIBING

**Capitalization:** Follow print for the use of capital letters. However, it is reasonable to reduce the use of capital letters in braille when they are used in print as a visual embellishment, such as for words written in capital letters at the beginning of paragraphs or chapters.

**Computer material:** Use contractions in computer material such as e-mail addresses, websites, URLs, and file names when it is embedded in regular text. Use uncontracted braille for computer material such as program code that may be displayed on separate lines, as well as any nearby excerpts from the program.

**Following print:** Follow the print whenever possible (with the exception of print ornamentation), including accents, punctuation, and capitalization.

**Punctuation:** Only one blank cell follows punctuation in braille even when print uses more space (for example, at the end of a sentence). If a punctuation mark appears in a position where it could be misread as a contraction, place a grade 1 symbol indicator (formerly known as the letter sign) before the punctuation mark.

**Saving space:** Choose formatting that uses the least amount of space while still maintaining the integrity or meaning of the print.

**Spacing:** Whenever there is some amount of space in print, including at the end of a line, there is a space in braille. If there is doubt as to whether a space is present in print, presume one is present. The amount of space present is not considered important. Indented paragraphs should be indented two spaces.

## TERMINOLOGY

**Alphabetic wordsign:** any one of the wordsigns in which a letter represents a word.

**Final-letter groupsign:** a two-cell braille sign formed by dots 4,6 or dots 5,6, followed by the final letter of the group.

**Groupsign:** a contraction that represents a group of letters.

**Indicator:** a braille sign that does not directly represent a print symbol but that indicates how subsequent braille sign(s) are to be interpreted.

**Initial-letter contraction:** a two-cell braille sign formed by dot 5; dots 4,5; or dots 4,5,6 followed by the first letter or groupsign of the word.

**Mode:** a condition initiated by an indicator and describing the effect of the indicator on subsequent braille signs.

**Passage:** three or more symbol sequences.

**Passage indicator:** initiates a mode which persists indefinitely until an explicit terminator is encountered.

**Prefix:** any one of the seven braille characters having only right-hand dots (⠈ ⠘ ⠸ ⠐ ⠨ ⠰ ⠠) or the braille character ⠦.

**Standing alone:** condition of being unaccompanied by additional letters, symbols, or punctuation except as specified in 2.6, the "standing alone" rule of *The Rules of Unified English Braille*; used to determine when a braille sign is read as a contraction.

**Strong:** designating contractions (other than alphabetic wordsigns) containing dots in both the top and bottom rows and in both the left and right columns of the braille cell.

**Strong character:** designating a braille character containing dots in both the top and bottom rows and in both the left and right columns of the braille cell, which therefore is physically unambiguous.

**Terminator:** a braille sign marking the end of a mode.

**Word indicator:** initiates a mode which extends over the next letter's sequence in the case of the capital's indicator or over the next symbol's sequence in the case of other indicators.

**Wordsign:** a contraction that represents a complete word.

## REFERENCE

Simpson, C. (Ed.). (2013). *The Rules of Unified English Braille* (2nd ed.). Lindisfarne, Australia: Round Table on Information Access for People with Print Disabilities Inc. and International Council on English Braille. Retrieved from http://www.iceb.org/ueb.html

# 2

# UEB Contractions at a Glance

This section displays the UEB literary braille letters and contractions alphabetically without any of the rules that pertain to them. The letters in parentheses have their own contractions, which can also be found within this section. No reference is made to the EBAE code in this section.

| Letter or Word | Contraction | Dot Configuration |
|---|---|---|
| a | • | (1) |
| about | ab | (1, 12) |
| above | abv | (1, 12, 1236) |
| according | ac | (1, 13) |
| across | acr | (1, 14, 1235) |
| after | af | (1, 124) |
| afternoon | afn | (1, 124, 1345) |
| afterward | afw | (1, 124, 2456) |
| again | ag | (1, 1245) |
| against | ag(st) | (1, 1245, 34) |
| almost | alm | (1, 123, 134) |
| already | alr | (1, 123, 1235) |
| also | al | (1, 123) |

| Letter or Word | Contraction | Dot Configuration |
|---|---|---|
| although | al(th) | (1, 123, 1456) |
| altogether | alt | (1, 123, 2345) |
| always | alw | (1, 123, 2456) |
| ance | ⠲⠢ | (46, 15) |
| and | ⠯ | (12346) |
| ar | ⠜ | (345) |
| as | z | (1356) |
| b | ⠃ | (12) |
| bb | ⠆ | (23) |
| be | ⠆ | (23) |
| because | (be)c | (23, 14) |
| before | (be)f | (23, 124) |
| behind | (be)h | (23, 125) |
| below | (be)l | (23, 123) |
| beneath | (be)n | (23, 1345) |
| beside | (be)s | (23, 234) |
| between | (be)t | (23, 2345) |
| beyond | (be)y | (23, 13456) |
| blind | bl | (12, 123) |
| braille | brl | (12, 1235, 123) |
| but | b | (12) |

| Letter or Word | Contraction | Dot Configuration |
|---|---|---|
| c | | (14) |
| can | c | (14) |
| cannot | | (456, 14) |
| cc | | (25) |
| ch | | (16) |
| character | | (5, 16) |
| child | | (16) |
| children | (ch)n | (16, 1345) |
| con | | (25) |
| conceive | (con)cv | (25, 14, 1236) |
| conceiving | (con)cvg | (25, 14, 1236, 1245) |
| could | cd | (14, 145) |
| d | | (145) |
| day | | (5, 145) |
| deceive | dcv | (145, 14, 1236) |
| deceiving | dcvg | (145, 14, 1236, 1245) |
| declare | dcl | (145, 14, 123) |
| declaring | dclg | (145, 14, 123, 1245) |
| dis | | (256) |

| Letter or Word | Contraction | Dot Configuration |
|---|---|---|
| do | d | (145) |
| e | ⠑ | (15) |
| ea | ⠂ | (2) |
| ed | ⠫ | (1246) |
| either | ei | (15, 24) |
| en | ⠢ | (26) |
| ence | ⠰⠑ | (56, 15) |
| enough | ⠢ | (26) |
| er | ⠻ | (12456) |
| ever | ⠐⠑ | (5, 15) |
| every | e | (15) |
| f | ⠋ | (124) |
| father | ⠐⠋ | (5, 124) |
| ff | ⠖ | (235) |
| first | f(st) | (124, 34) |
| for | ⠿ | (123456) |
| friend | fr | (124, 1235) |
| from | f | (124) |

| Letter or Word | Contraction | Dot Configuration |
|---|---|---|
| ful | ⠒⠿ | (56, 123) |
| g | ⠛ | (1245) |
| gg | ⠶ | (2356) |
| gh | ⠣ | (126) |
| go | g | (1245) |
| good | gd | (1245, 145) |
| great | grt | (1245, 1235, 2345) |
| h | ⠓ | (125) |
| had | ⠸⠓ | (456, 125) |
| have | h | (125) |
| here | ⠐⠓ | (5, 125) |
| herself | h(er)f | (125, 12456, 124) |
| him | hm | (125, 134) |
| himself | hmf | (125, 134, 124) |
| his | ⠦ | (236) |
| i | ⠊ | (24) |
| immediate | imm | (24, 134, 134) |
| in | ⠔ | (35) |

| Letter or Word | Contraction | Dot Configuration |
|---|---|---|
| ing | | (346) |
| it | x | (1346) |
| its | xs | (1346, 234) |
| itself | xf | (1346, 124) |
| ity | | (56, 13456) |
| j | | (245) |
| just | j | (245) |
| k | | (13) |
| know | | (5, 13) |
| knowledge | k | (13) |
| l | | (123) |
| less | | (46, 234) |
| letter | lr | (123, 1235) |
| like | l | (123) |
| little | ll | (123, 123) |
| lord | | (5, 123) |
| m | | (134) |
| many | | (456, 134) |

| Letter or Word | Contraction | Dot Configuration |
|---|:---:|---|
| ment | ⠀ | (56, 2345) |
| more | m | (134) |
| mother | ⠀ | (5, 134) |
| much | m(ch) | (134, 16) |
| must | m(st) | (134, 34) |
| myself | myf | (134, 13456, 124) |
| n | ⠝ | (1345) |
| name | ⠀ | (5, 1345) |
| necessary | nec | (1345, 15, 14) |
| neither | nei | (1345, 15, 24) |
| ness | ⠀ | (56, 234) |
| not | n | (1345) |
| o | ⠕ | (135) |
| of | ⠿ | (12356) |
| one | ⠀ | (5, 135) |
| oneself | (one)f | (5, 135, 124) |
| ong | ⠀ | (56, 1245) |
| ou | ⠳ | (1256) |

| Letter or Word | Contraction | Dot Configuration |
|---|---|---|
| ought | ⠪ | (5, 1256) |
| ound | ⠪ | (46, 145) |
| ount | ⠪ | (46, 2345) |
| ourselves | (ou)rvs | (1256, 1235, 1236, 234) |
| out | ⠳ | (1256) |
| ow | ⠪ | (246) |
| p | ⠏ | (1234) |
| paid | pd | (1234, 145) |
| part | ⠰⠏ | (5, 1234) |
| people | p | (1234) |
| perceive | p(er)cv | (1234, 12456, 14, 1236) |
| perceiving | p(er)cvg | (1234, 12456, 14, 1236, 1245) |
| perhaps | p(er)h | (1234, 12456, 125) |
| q | ⠟ | (12345) |
| question | ⠐⠟ | (5, 12345) |
| quick | qk | (12345, 13) |
| quite | q | (12345) |

| Letter or Word | Contraction | Dot Configuration |
|---|---|---|
| r | | (1235) |
| rather | r | (1235) |
| receive | rcv | (1235, 14, 1236) |
| receiving | rcvg | (1235, 14, 1236, 1245) |
| rejoice | rjc | (1235, 245, 14) |
| rejoicing | rjcg | (1235, 245, 14, 1245) |
| right | | (5, 1235) |
| s | | (234) |
| said | sd | (234, 145) |
| sh | | (146) |
| shall | | (146) |
| should | (sh)d | (146, 145) |
| sion | | (46, 1345) |
| so | s | (234) |
| some | | (5, 234) |
| spirit | | (456, 234) |
| st | | (34) |
| still | | (34) |

| Letter or Word | Contraction | Dot Configuration |
|---|---|---|
| such | s(ch) | (234, 16) |
| t | ⠞ | (2345) |
| th | ⠹ | (1456) |
| that | t | (2345) |
| the | ⠮ | (2346) |
| their | ⠸⠮ | (456, 2346) |
| themselves | (the)mvs | (2346, 134, 1236, 234) |
| there | ⠐⠮ | (5, 2346) |
| these | ⠘⠮ | (45, 2346) |
| this | ⠹ | (1456) |
| those | ⠘⠹ | (45, 1456) |
| through | ⠐⠹ | (5, 1456) |
| thyself | (th)yf | (1456, 13456, 124) |
| time | ⠐⠞ | (5, 2345) |
| tion | ⠰⠝ | (56, 1345) |
| today | td | (2345, 145) |
| together | tgr | (2345, 1245, 1235) |

| Letter or Word | Contraction | Dot Configuration |
|---|---|---|
| tomorrow | tm | (2345, 134) |
| tonight | tn | (2345, 1345) |
| u | ⠄ | (136) |
| under | ⠄ | (5, 136) |
| upon | ⠄ | (45, 136) |
| us | u | (136) |
| v | ⠄ | (1236) |
| very | v | (1236) |
| w | ⠄ | (2456) |
| was | ⠄ | (356) |
| were | ⠄ | (2356) |
| wh | ⠄ | (156) |
| where | ⠄ | (5, 156) |
| which | ⠄ | (156) |
| whose | ⠄ | (45, 156) |
| will | w | (2456) |
| with | ⠄ | (23456) |

| Letter or Word | Contraction | Dot Configuration |
|---|---|---|
| word | ⠺⠙ | (45, 2456) |
| work | ⠢⠅ | (5, 2456) |
| world | ⠺⠙ | (456, 2456) |
| would | wd | (2456, 145) |
| x | ⠭ | (1346) |
| y | ⠽ | (13456) |
| you | y | (13456) |
| young | ⠢⠽ | (5, 13456) |
| your | yr | (13456, 1235) |
| yourself | yrf | (13456, 1235, 124) |
| yourselves | yrvs | (13456, 1235, 1236, 234) |
| z | ⠵ | (1356) |

# 3

# Punctuation, Symbols, and Indicators

| | Print Symbol | Braille Symbol | UEB Rule Number |
|---|---|---|---|
| accent, acute | ´ (é) | ⠘⠌ | 4.2 |
| accent, tilde (modifier) | ~ (ñ) | ⠘⠹ | 4.1 |
| ampersand | & | ⠈⠯ | 3.1 |
| apostrophe | ' | ⠄ | 7.0 |
| asterisk | * | ⠐⠔ | 3.3 |
| at sign | @ | ⠈⠁ | 3.7 |
| backslash | \ | ⠸⠡ | 7.0 |
| bold, passage | you can go | ⠘⠶ | 9.4 |
| bold, symbol | b | ⠘⠂ | 9.2 |
| bold, terminator | | ⠘⠄ | 9.4 |

17

|  | Print Symbol | Braille Symbol | UEB Rule Number |
|---|---|---|---|
| bold, word | read | ⠼ | 9.3 |
| brackets, angle | < > | | 7.0 |
| brackets, curly | { } | | 7.0 |
| brackets, square | [ ] | | 7.0 |
| braille grouping open and close | | | 3.4 |
| bullet | • | | 3.5 |
| capital, letter | B | | 8.0 |
| capital, passage | YOU CAN GO | | 8.5 |
| capital, terminator | | | 8.6 |
| capital, word | READ | | 8.4 |
| caret | ^ | | 3.6 |
| colon | : | | 7.0 |
| comma | , | | 7.0 |
| dash | – | | 7.2 |
| degree | ° | | 3.11 |

|  | Print Symbol | Braille Symbol | UEB Rule Number |
|---|---|---|---|
| divided by | ÷ | ⠐⠌ | 3.17 |
| dollar sign | $ | ⠈⠎ | 3.10 |
| ellipsis | . . . | ⠲⠲⠲ | 7.3 |
| equals | = | ⠐⠶ | 3.17 |
| exclamation mark | ! | ⠖ | 7.0 |
| grade 1, passage |  | ⠰⠰⠰ | 5.4 |
| grade 1, symbol (letter sign) |  | ⠰ | 5.2 |
| grade 1, terminator |  | ⠰⠄ | 5.5 |
| grade 1, word |  | ⠰⠰ | 5.3 |
| greater than | > | ⠈⠣ | 3.17 |
| guide dot | . . . . . | ⠄⠄⠄ | 16.5 |
| hashtag, pound sign, number sign | # | ⠸⠹ | 3.19 |
| hyphen | - | ⠤ | 7.2 |
| italic, passage | *you can go* | ⠨⠶ | 9.4 |

| | Print Symbol | Braille Symbol | UEB Rule Number |
|---|---|---|---|
| italic, symbol | *b* | | 9.2 |
| italic, terminator | | | 9.4 |
| italic, word | *read* | | 9.3 |
| less than | < | | 3.17 |
| level change down, subscript, base | $\square_1$ | | 3.24 |
| level change up, superscript, exponent, power | $\square^2$ | | 3.24 |
| long dash | — | | 7.2 |
| minus | – | | 3.17 |
| multiplication | x | | 3.17 |
| numeric indicator | | | 5.6 |
| numeric passage indicator | | | 6.9 |
| numeric terminator | | | 6.9 |
| parentheses | ( ) | | 7.0 |

| | Print Symbol | Braille Symbol | UEB Rule Number |
|---|---|---|---|
| percent | % | ⠨⠴ | 3.21 |
| period, dot, decimal | . | ⠲ | 7.0 |
| plus | + | ⠐⠖ | 3.17 |
| question mark | ? | ⠦ | 7.5 |
| quotation mark, double | ” “ | ⠦  ⠴ | 7.6 |
| quotation mark, single | ’ ‘ | ⠠⠦  ⠠⠴ | 7.6 |
| semicolon | ; | ⠆ | 7.0 |
| slash, forward (solidus) | / | ⠸⠌ | 7.4 |
| tilde (swung dash) | ~ | ⠈⠔ | 3.25 |
| transcriber's note | | ⠰⠂⠄  ⠠⠄⠆ | 3.27 |
| underline, passage | <u>you can go</u> | ⠸⠶ | 9.4 |
| underline, symbol | <u>b</u> | ⠸⠆ | 9.2 |
| underline, terminator | | ⠸⠄ | 9.4 |
| underline, word | <u>read</u> | ⠸⠒ | 9.3 |
| underscore | _ | ⠨⠤ | 7.2 |

# 4

## Braille to Print

This section displays all the braille symbols and contractions numerically. It also includes a brief description of where they may appear in text.

The section is organized in numerical fashion on the basis of the six-dot cell system. The dots are designated as follows:

**THE BRAILLE CELL**

$$
\begin{array}{ccc}
1 & \bullet\ \bullet & 4 \\
2 & \bullet\ \bullet & 5 \\
3 & \bullet\ \bullet & 6
\end{array}
$$

The symbols in this section are grouped according to the number of cells the symbol uses and the number of dots used in the first cell. Within these subcategories (number of cells, number of dots), the symbols are organized numerically in ascending order beginning with the first cell. For example, in the subcategory 1 CELL, 2 DOTS, the symbols are in the following order:

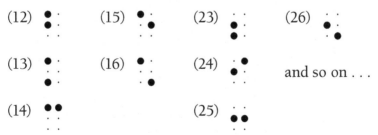

When there is a symbol that was used in English Braille, American Edition (EBAE), but is not used in Unified English Braille (UEB), its description will be followed by the notation [EBAE code].

## 1 CELL, 1 DOT

(1)

**a**

1    (when preceded by the numeric indicator)

(2)

**ea**    Groupsign only. Will be found in the middle of the word only.

,    Comma.

(3)

'    Apostrophe.

(4)

Prefix, e.g. when found before a (@), c (¢), e (€), y (¥), or ampersand (&).

`    Accent. [EBAE code]

(5)

Prefix, begins initial-letter contraction. Numeric space when found within a number.

(6)

Capitalization indicator.

Prefix.

## 1 CELL, 2 DOTS

(12)

**b**

**but**    Alphabetic wordsign. May be used as a wordsign only.

2    (when preceded by the numeric indicator)

(13)

k

**knowledge**   Alphabetic wordsign. May be used as a wordsign only.

(14)

c

**can**   Alphabetic wordsign. May be used as a wordsign only.
3   (when preceded by the numeric indicator)

(15)

e

**every**   Alphabetic wordsign. May be used as a wordsign only.
5   (when preceded by the numeric indicator)

(16)

**ch**   Groupsign.
**child**   Wordsign only. May be followed by an apostrophe.

(23)

**be**   Groupsign or wordsign.
**bb**   Groupsign. Will be found in the middle of the word only.
;   Semicolon.

(24)

i

9   (when preceded by the numeric indicator)

**(25)**

**con**   Groupsign.

**cc**   Groupsign. Will be found in the middle of the word only.

**:**   Colon.

**(26)**

**en**   Groupsign.

**enough**   Wordsign only.

Level change down (subscript, base) when preceded by prefix dots 56.

**(34)**

**st**   Groupsign or abbreviation.

**still**   Wordsign only. May be followed by an apostrophe.

**/**   Solidus (forward slash) when preceded by dots 456.

**/**   Slash. [EBAE code]

**(35)**

**in**   Groupsign or wordsign.

Level change up (superscript, exponent, power) when preceded by prefix dots 56.

**(36)**

**-**   Hyphen.

**com**   Groupsign. [EBAE code]

Dash when sign is doubled. [EBAE code]

**(45)**

Prefix.

**(46)**

Prefix.

Italic, underline, or bold sign. [EBAE code]

**.**   Decimal point. [EBAE code]

(56)

**Grade 1 symbol indicator**    Formerly called the letter sign.
Prefix, begins a groupsign, final-letter contraction.

## 1 CELL, 3 DOTS

(123)

l

**like**    Alphabetic wordsign. May be used as a wordsign only.

(124)

f

**from**    Alphabetic wordsign. May be used as a wordsign only.
6    (when preceded by the numeric indicator)

(125)

h

**have**    Alphabetic wordsign. May be used as a wordsign only.
8    (when preceded by the numeric indicator)

(126)

**gh**    Groupsign only.

(134)

m

**more**    Alphabetic wordsign. May be used as a wordsign only.

(135)

o

(136)

u

**us**   Alphabetic wordsign. May be used as a wordsign only.

(145)

d

**do**   Alphabetic wordsign. May be used as a wordsign only.

4   (when preceded by the numeric indicator)

(146)

**sh**   Groupsign.

**shall**   Wordsign only.

(156)

**wh**   Groupsign.

**which**   Wordsign only.

(234)

s

**so**   Alphabetic wordsign. May be used as a wordsign only.

(235)

**ff**   Groupsign. Will be found in the middle of the word only.

!   Exclamation mark.

**to**   Wordsign only. There will be no space between this symbol and the word, composition sign, or symbol that follows. [EBAE code]

**(236)**
**his**   Wordsign only.
?   Question mark.
"   Opening quotation mark.

**(245)**
**j**
**just**   Alphabetic wordsign. May be used as a wordsign only.
0   (zero, when preceded by a numeric indicator)

**(246)**
**ow**   Groupsign.

**(256)**
**dis**   Groupsign.
.   Period, decimal, or dot.
**dd**   Groupsign. [EBAE code]
$   Dollar sign. [EBAE code]

**(345)**
**ar**   Groupsign.

**(346)**
**ing**   Groupsign.

**(356)**
**was**   Wordsign only.
"   Closing quotation mark.
**by**   Wordsign only. There will be no space between this symbol and the word, composition sign, or symbol that follows. [EBAE code]

**(456)**
Prefix, begins a groupsign or a wordsign.

## 1 CELL, 4 DOTS

**(1234)**

**p**

**people**   Alphabetic wordsign. May be used as a wordsign only.

**(1235)**

**r**

**rather**   Alphabetic wordsign. May be used as a wordsign only.

**(1236)**

**v**

**very**   Alphabetic wordsign. May be used as a wordsign only.

**(1245)**

**g**

**go**   Alphabetic wordsign. May be used as a wordsign only.

**7**   (when preceded by the numeric indicator)

**(1246)**

**ed**   Groupsign.

**(1256)**

**ou**   Groupsign.

**out**   Wordsign only.

**(1345)**

**n**

**not**   Alphabetic wordsign. May be used as a wordsign only.

(1346)

x

**it** Alphabetic wordsign. May be used as a wordsign only.

(1356)

z

**as** Alphabetic wordsign. May be used as a wordsign only.

(1456)
**th** Groupsign.
**this** Wordsign only.

(2345)

t

**that** Alphabetic wordsign. May be used as a wordsign only.

(2346)
**the** Groupsign or wordsign.

(2356)
**were** Wordsign only.
**gg** Groupsign. Will be found in the middle of the word only.
( Opening parenthesis. [EBAE code]
) Closing parenthesis. [EBAE code]
[ Opening bracket. [EBAE code]
] Closing bracket. [EBAE code]

(2456)

w

**will** Alphabetic wordsign. May be used as a wordsign only.

(3456)
Numeric indicator.
**ble**   Groupsign. [EBAE code]

## 1 CELL, 5 DOTS

(12345)
q
**quite**   Alphabetic wordsign. May be used as a wordsign only.

(12346)
**and**   Groupsign or wordsign.

(12356)
**of**   Groupsign or wordsign.

(12456)
**er**   Groupsign.

(13456)
y
**you**   Alphabetic wordsign. May be used as a wordsign only.

(23456)
**with**   Groupsign or wordsign.

## 1 CELL, 6 DOTS

(123456)
**for**   Groupsign or wordsign.

## 2 CELLS, 1 DOT

(1, 12)
**about**   Shortform. May be used as a word or part of a longer word.

(1, 14)
**according**   Shortform. May be used as a word or part of a longer word.

(1, 123)
**also**   Shortform. May be used as a word or part of a longer word.

(1, 124)
**after**   Shortform. May be used as a word or part of a longer word.

(1, 1245)
**again**   Shortform. May be used as a word or part of a longer word.

(5, 13)
**know**   Groupsign or wordsign.

(5, 15)
**ever**   Groupsign or wordsign.

(5, 16)
**character**   Groupsign or wordsign.

(5, 123)
**lord**   Groupsign or wordsign.

(5, 124)
**father**   Groupsign or wordsign.

(5, 125)
**here**   Groupsign or wordsign.

(5, 134)
**mother**   Groupsign or wordsign.

(5, 135)
**one**   Groupsign or wordsign.

(5, 136)
**under**   Groupsign or wordsign.

(5, 145)
**day** Groupsign or wordsign.

(5, 156)
**where** Groupsign or wordsign.

(5, 234)
**some** Groupsign or wordsign.

(5, 1234)
**part** Groupsign or wordsign.

(5, 1235)
**right** Groupsign or wordsign.

(5, 1256)
**ought** Groupsign or wordsign.

(5, 1345)
**name** Groupsign or wordsign.

(5, 1456)
**through** Groupsign or wordsign.

(5, 2345)
**time** Groupsign or wordsign.

(5, 2346)
**there** Groupsign or wordsign.

(5, 2456)
**work** Groupsign or wordsign.

(5, 12345)
**question** Groupsign or wordsign.

(5, 13456)
**young** Groupsign or wordsign.

(6, 3)

Capitals terminator.

General termination sign. [EBAE code]

(6, 1345)

**ation**   Groupsign. [EBAE code]

(6, 13456)

**ally**   Groupsign. [EBAE code]

(6, 2356)

[   Bracket/brace (opening). [EBAE code]

## 2 CELLS, 2 DOTS

(12, 123)

**blind**   Shortform. May be used as a word or part of a longer word.

(14, 145)

**could**   Shortform. May be used as a word or part of a longer word.

(15, 24)

**either**   Shortform. May be used as a word or part of a longer word.

(16, 1345)

**children**   Shortform. May be used as a word or part of a longer word.

(23, 14)

**because**   Shortform. May be used as a word or part of a longer word.

(23, 123)

**below**   Shortform. May be used as a word or part of a longer word.

(23, 124)
**before**   Shortform. May be used as a word or part of a longer word.

(23, 125)
**behind**   Shortform. May be used as a word or part of a longer word.

(23, 234)
**beside**   Shortform. May be used as a word or part of a longer word.

(23, 1345)
**beneath**   Shortform. May be used as a word or part of a longer word.

(23, 2345)
**between**   Shortform. May be used as a word or part of a longer word.

(23, 13456)
**beyond**   Shortform. May be used as a word or part of a longer word.

(25, 1234)
%   Percent. [EBAE code]

(35, 35)
*   Asterisk. [EBAE code]

(35, 235)
**into**   Wordsign only. There will be no space between this symbol and the word, composition sign, or symbol that follows. [EBAE code]

(45, 136)
**upon**   Groupsign or wordsign.

(45, 156)
**whose**    Groupsign or wordsign.

(45, 1456)
**those**    Groupsign or wordsign.

(45, 2346)
**these**    Groupsign or wordsign.

(45, 2456)
**word**    Groupsign or wordsign.

(46, 15)
**ance**    Groupsign.

(46, 145)
**ound**    Groupsign.

(46, 234)
**less**    Groupsign.

(46, 1345)
**sion**    Groupsign.

(46, 2345)
**ount**    Groupsign.

(56, 15)
**ence**    Groupsign.

(56, 123)
**ful**    Groupsign.

(56, 234)
**ness**    Groupsign.

(56, 1245)
**ong**    Groupsign.

(56, 1345)
**tion**   Groupsign.

(56, 2345)
**ment**   Groupsign.

(56, 13456)
**ity**   Groupsign.

## 2 CELLS, 3 DOTS

(123, 123)
**little**   Shortform. May be used as a word or part of a longer word.

(123, 1235)
**letter**   Shortform. May be used as a word or part of a longer word.

(124, 34)
**first**   Shortform. May be used as a word or part of a longer word.

(124, 1235)
**friend**   Shortform. May be used as a word or part of a longer word.

(125, 134)
**him**   Shortform. May be used as a word or part of a longer word.

(134, 16)
**much**   Shortform. May be used as a word or part of a longer word.

(134, 34)
**must**   Shortform. May be used as a word or part of a longer word.

**(146, 145)**
**should** Shortform. May be used as a word or part of a longer word.

**(234, 16)**
**such** Shortform. May be used as a word or part of a longer word.

**(234, 145)**
**said** Shortform. May be used as a word or part of a longer word.

**(456, 14)**
**cannot** Groupsign or whole word contraction.

**(456, 125)**
**had** Groupsign or whole word contraction.

**(456, 134)**
**many** Groupsign or whole word contraction.

**(456, 1456)**
**#** Hashtag, pound sign, printed number sign.

**(456, 234)**
**spirit** Groupsign or whole word contraction.

**(456, 2346)**
**their** Groupsign or whole word contraction.

(456, 2456)
**world**    Groupsign or whole word contraction.

---

## 2 CELLS, 4 DOTS

(1234, 145)
**paid**    Shortform. May be used as a word or part of a longer word.

(1245, 145)
**good**    Shortform. May be used as a word or part of a longer word.

(1346, 124)
**itself**    Shortform. May be used as a word or part of a longer word.

(1346, 234)
**its**    Shortform. May be used as a word or part of a longer word.

(2345, 134)
**tomorrow**    Shortform. May be used as a word or part of a longer word.

(2345, 145)
**today**    Shortform. May be used as a word or part of a longer word.

(2345, 1345)
**tonight**    Shortform. May be used as a word or part of a longer word.

(2356, 3)
]    Bracket/brace (closing). [EBAE code]

 (2456, 145)

**would** Shortform. May be used as a word or part of a longer word.

## 2 CELLS, 5 DOTS

(12345, 13)

**quick** Shortform. May be used as a word or part of a longer word.

(13456, 1235)

**your** Shortform. May be used as a word or part of a longer word.

## 3 CELLS, 1 DOT

(1, 12, 1236)

**above** Shortform. May be used as a word or part of a longer word.

(1, 14, 1235)

**across** Shortform. May be used as a word or part of a longer word.

(1, 123, 134)

**almost** Shortform. May be used as a word or part of a longer word.

(1, 123, 1235)

**already** Shortform. May be used as a word or part of a longer word.

(1, 123, 1456)

**although** Shortform. May be used as a word or part of a longer word.

(1, 123, 2345)

**altogether** Shortform. May be used as a word or part of a longer word.

(1, 123, 2456)
**always**   Shortform. May be used as a word or part of a longer word.

(1, 124, 1345)
**afternoon**   Shortform. May be used as a word or part of a longer word.

(1, 124, 2456)
**afterward**   Shortform. May be used as a word or part of a longer word.

(1, 1245, 34)
**against**   Shortform. May be used as a word or part of a longer word.

(3, 3, 3)
. . .   Ellipsis. [EBAE code]

(5, 135, 124)
**oneself**   Shortform. May be used as a word or part of a longer word.

## 3 CELLS, 2 DOTS

(12, 1235, 123)
**braille**   Shortform. May be used as a word or part of a longer word.

(24, 134, 134)
**immediate**   Shortform. May be used as a word or part of a longer word.

(25, 14, 1236)
**conceive**   Shortform. May be used as a word or part of a longer word.

## 3 CELLS, 3 DOTS

(125, 134, 124)

**himself**   Shortform. May be used as a word or part of a longer word.

(125, 12456, 124)

**herself**   Shortform. May be used as a word or part of a longer word.

(134, 13456, 124)

**myself**   Shortform. May be used as a word or part of a longer word.

(135, 3, 14)

**o'clock**   Shortform. May be used as a word or part of a longer word. [EBAE code]

(145, 14, 123)

**declare**   Shortform. May be used as a word or part of a longer word.

(145, 14, 1236)

**deceive**   Shortform. May be used as a word or part of a longer word.

## 3 CELLS, 4 DOTS

(1234, 12456, 125)

**perhaps**   Shortform. May be used as a word or part of a longer word.

(1235, 14, 1236)

**receive**   Shortform. May be used as a word or part of a longer word.

(1235, 245, 14)

**rejoice**   Shortform. May be used as a word or part of a longer word.

(1245, 1235, 2345)

**great**   Shortform. May be used as a word or part of a longer word.

(1345, 15, 14)

**necessary**   Shortform. May be used as a word or part of a longer word.

(1345, 15, 24)

**neither**   Shortform. May be used as a word or part of a longer word.

(1456, 13456, 124)

**thyself**   Shortform. May be used as a word or part of a longer word.

(2345, 1245, 1235)

**together**   Shortform. May be used as a word or part of a longer word.

## 3 CELLS, 5 DOTS

(13456, 1235, 124)

**yourself**   Shortform. May be used as a word or part of a longer word.

## 4 CELLS, 2 DOTS

(25, 14, 1236, 1245)

**conceiving**   Shortform. May be used as a word or part of a longer word.

## 4 CELLS, 3 DOTS

(145, 14, 123, 1245)

**declaring**   Shortform. May be used as a word or part of a longer word.

(145, 14, 1236, 1245)

**deceiving**   Shortform. May be used as a word or part of a longer word.

## 4 CELLS, 4 DOTS

(1234, 12456, 14, 1236)
**perceive** Shortform. May be used as a word or part of a longer word.

(1235, 14, 1236, 1245)
**receiving** Shortform. May be used as a word or part of a longer word.

(1235, 245, 14, 1245)
**rejoicing** Shortform. May be used as a word or part of a longer word.

(1256, 1235, 1236, 234)
**ourselves** Shortform. May be used as a word or part of a longer word.

(2346, 134, 1236, 234)
**themselves** Shortform. May be used as a word or part of a longer word.

## 4 CELLS, 5 DOTS

(13456, 1235, 1236, 234)
**yourselves** Shortform. May be used as a word or part of a longer word.

## 5 CELLS, 4 DOTS

(1234, 12456, 14, 1236, 1245)
**perceiving** Shortform. May be used as a word or part of a longer word.

# 5

# Print to Braille

This section alphabetically lists all common literary contractions and symbols used in braille and briefly describes the rules that pertain to them. Not all of the rules are included here; only those that are commonly used have been included.

This section contains only the UEB code and makes no reference to the EBAE code.

## a – dot 1

Letter, wordsign, stand-alone.

## about – ab

Shortform, stand-alone contraction. May be used as a proper name. Use a grade 1 indicator if a letter sequence could be confused with a shortform (whole or part). May be followed by an 's. May not be followed by an s.

May be used as part of a longer word as long as the entire word is standing alone and if the longer word appears on the UEB Shortforms List.

## above – abv

Shortform, stand-alone contraction. May be used as a proper name. Use a grade 1 indicator if a letter sequence could be confused with a shortform (whole or part). May be followed by an s or an 's.

May be used as part of a longer word as long as the entire word is standing alone and if the longer word appears on the UEB Short-forms List.

### according – ac

Shortform, stand-alone contraction. May be used as a proper name. Use a grade 1 indicator if a letter sequence could be confused with a shortform (whole or part). May be followed by an s or an 's.

May be used as part of a longer word as long as the entire word is standing alone and if the longer word appears on the UEB Short-forms List.

### across – acr

Shortform, stand-alone contraction. May be used as a proper name. Use a grade 1 indicator if a letter sequence could be confused with a shortform (whole or part). May be followed by an s or an 's.

May be used as part of a longer word as long as the entire word is standing alone and if the longer word appears on the UEB Short-forms List.

### after – af

Shortform, stand-alone contraction. May be used as a proper name. Use a grade 1 indicator if a letter sequence could be confused with a shortform (whole or part). May be followed by an s or an 's.

May be used as part of a longer word as long as the entire word is standing alone and if the longer word appears on the UEB Short-forms List.

### afternoon – afn

Shortform, stand-alone contraction. May be used as a proper name. Use a grade 1 indicator if a letter sequence could be confused with a shortform (whole or part). May be followed by an s or an 's.

May be used as part of a longer word as long as the entire word is standing alone and if the longer word appears on the UEB Short-forms List.

### afterward – afw

Shortform, stand-alone contraction. May be used as a proper name. Use a grade 1 indicator if a letter sequence could be confused with a shortform (whole or part). May be followed by an *s* or an *'s*.

May be used as part of a longer word as long as the entire word is standing alone and if the longer word appears on the UEB Short-forms List.

### again – ag

Shortform, stand-alone contraction. May be used as a proper name. Use a grade 1 indicator if a letter sequence could be confused with a shortform (whole or part). May be followed by an *s* or an *'s*.

May be used as part of a longer word as long as the entire word is standing alone and if the longer word appears on the UEB Short-forms List.

### against – ag(st)

Shortform, stand-alone contraction. May be used as a proper name. May be followed by an *s* or an *'s*.

May be used as part of a longer word as long as the entire word is standing alone and if the longer word appears on the UEB Short-forms List.

### almost – alm

Shortform, stand-alone contraction. May be used as a proper name. Use a grade 1 indicator if a letter sequence could be confused with a shortform (whole or part). May be followed by an *'s*. May not be followed by an *s*.

May be used as part of a longer word as long as the entire word is standing alone and if the longer word appears on the UEB Short-forms List.

### already – alr

Shortform, stand-alone contraction. May be used as a proper name. Use a grade 1 indicator if a letter sequence could be confused with a shortform (whole or part). May be followed by an *s* or an *'s*.

May be used as part of a longer word as long as the entire word is standing alone and if the longer word appears on the UEB Short-forms List.

### also – al

Shortform, stand-alone contraction. May be used as a proper name. Use a grade 1 indicator if a letter sequence could be confused with a shortform (whole or part). May be followed by an *s* or an *'s*.

May be used as part of a longer word as long as the entire word is standing alone and if the longer word appears on the UEB Short-forms List.

### although – al(th)

Shortform, stand-alone contraction. May be used as a proper name. May be followed by an *s* or an *'s*.

May be used as part of a longer word as long as the entire word is standing alone and if the longer word appears on the UEB Short-forms List.

### altogether – alt

Shortform, stand-alone contraction. May be used as a proper name. Use a grade 1 indicator if a letter sequence could be confused with a shortform (whole or part). May be followed by an *s* or an *'s*.

May be used as part of a longer word as long as the entire word is standing alone and if the longer word appears on the UEB Short-forms List.

### always – alw

Shortform, stand-alone contraction. May be used as a proper name. Use a grade 1 indicator if a letter sequence could be confused with a shortform (whole or part). May be followed by an *s* or an *'s*.

May be used as part of a longer word as long as the entire word is standing alone and if the longer word appears on the UEB Shortforms List.

### ance – dots (46, 15)

Final-letter groupsign. Can be used only in the middle or at the end of a word. Must follow a letter, a contraction, a modified letter, or a ligatured letter. May directly follow a prefix. May not begin a new line in a divided word.

### and – dots (12346)

Wordsign, strong contraction. Must be preceded and followed by a space within a sentence. May be preceded or followed by punctuation.

Groupsign. Can be used as a groupsign wherever the letters occur except where rules limit their use. Can be used when separated by a prefix/suffix and a root. Cannot be used when separated by components of compound words.

### ar – dots (345)

Groupsign. Can be used in contact with punctuation, including a hyphen and an apostrophe. Can be used when separated by a prefix/suffix and a root. Cannot be used when separated by components of compound words.

### as – z

Alphabetic wordsign, stand-alone, wordsign only. Can be used in contact with punctuation, including a hyphen. Can be used in contact with an apostrophe when the letters following are: *'d, 'll, 're, 's, 't,* or *'ve*.

## b – dots (12) ⠃

Must be preceded by a grade 1 indicator (letter sign) when representing a single letter.

## bb – dots (23) ⠆

Lower groupsign. Can be used only between letters or contractions within a word. Cannot be preceded or followed by a capital indicator/terminator. All other one-cell contractions have precedence.

## be – dots (23) ⠆

Lower wordsign. Can be used when the word it represents is standing alone. Cannot be used when in contact with any punctuation sign, including the hyphen and dash, which has only lower dots. The capital indicator/terminator does not negate this rule.

Lower groupsign. Used only in the first syllable of a word. May be preceded by a hyphen or dash. Cannot be followed by a capital indicator/terminator.

## because – (be)c

Shortform, stand-alone contraction. May be used as a proper name. Use a grade 1 indicator if a letter sequence could be confused with a shortform (whole or part). May be followed by an s or an 's.

May be used as part of a longer word as long as the entire word is standing alone and if the longer word appears on the UEB Shortforms List.

## before – (be)f

Shortform, stand-alone contraction. May be used as a proper name. May be followed by an s or an 's.

May be used as part of a longer word as long as the entire word is standing alone and if the longer word appears on the UEB Shortforms List.

## behind – (be)h

Shortform, stand-alone contraction. May be used as a proper name. May be followed by an *s* or an *'s*.

May be used as part of a longer word as long as the entire word is standing alone and if the longer word appears on the UEB Short-forms List.

## below – (be)l

Shortform, stand-alone contraction. May be used as a proper name. May be followed by an *s* or an *'s*.

May be used as part of a longer word as long as the entire word is standing alone and if the longer word appears on the UEB Short-forms List.

## beneath – (be)n

Shortform, stand-alone contraction. May be used as a proper name. May be followed by an *s* or an *'s*.

May be used as part of a longer word as long as the entire word is standing alone and if the longer word appears on the UEB Short-forms List.

## beside – (be)s

Shortform, stand-alone contraction. May be used as a proper name. May be followed by an *s* or an *'s*.

May be used as part of a longer word as long as the entire word is standing alone and if the longer word appears on the UEB Short-forms List.

## between – (be)t

Shortform, stand-alone contraction. May be used as a proper name. May be followed by an *s* or an *'s*.

May be used as part of a longer word as long as the entire word is standing alone and if the longer word appears on the UEB Short-forms List.

### beyond – (be)y

Shortform, stand-alone contraction. May be used as a proper name. May be followed by an *s* or an *'s*.

May be used as part of a longer word as long as the entire word is standing alone and if the longer word appears on the UEB Short-forms List.

### blind – bl

Shortform, stand-alone contraction. May be used as a proper name. Use a grade 1 indicator if a letter sequence could be confused with a shortform (whole or part). May be followed by an *s* or an *'s*.

May be used as part of a longer word. The longer word does not need to appear on the Shortforms List as long as the entire word is standing alone (including any affix with an apostrophe), the short-form begins the word, and it is not followed by a vowel or *y*.

### braille – brl

Shortform, stand-alone contraction. May be used as a proper name. Use a grade 1 indicator if a letter sequence could be confused with a shortform (whole or part). May be followed by an *s* or an *'s*.

May be used as part of a longer word as long as the entire word is standing alone. The longer word does not need to appear on the Shortforms List as long as the entire word is standing alone (including any affix with an apostrophe).

### but – b

Alphabetic wordsign, stand-alone, wordsign only. Can be used in contact with punctuation, including a hyphen. Can be used in contact with an apostrophe when the letters following are: *'d, 'll, 're, 's, 't,* or *'ve.*

# c – dots (14) ⠉

Must be preceded by a grade 1 indicator (letter sign) when representing a single letter.

## can – c

Alphabetic wordsign, stand-alone, wordsign only. Can be used in contact with punctuation, including a hyphen. Can be used in contact with an apostrophe when the letters following are: 'd, 'll, 're, 's, 't, or 've.

## cannot – dots (456, 14) ⠸⠉

Initial-letter contraction. Can be used as a groupsign or a wordsign.

## cc – dots (25) ⠒

Lower groupsign. Can be used only between letters or contractions within a word. Cannot be preceded or followed by a capital indicator/terminator. All other one-cell contractions have precedence.

## ch – dots (16) ⠡

Groupsign. Can be used in contact with punctuation, including a hyphen and an apostrophe. Can be used when separated by a prefix/suffix and a root. Cannot be used when separated by components of compound words. Cannot be used when the c and the h are pronounced separately.

## character – dots (5, 16) ⠐⠡

Initial-letter contraction. Can be used as a groupsign or a wordsign.

## child – (ch)

Wordsign, stand-alone. Can be used in contact with punctuation and composition signs. Can be used in contact with an apostrophe when the letters following are: 'd, 'll, 're, 's, 't, or 've.

## children – (ch)n

Shortform, stand-alone contraction. May be used as a proper name. May be followed by an *s* or an *'s*.

May be used as a part of a longer word. The longer word does not need to appear on the Shortforms List as long as the entire word is standing alone (including any affix with an apostrophe). May not be followed by a vowel or *y*.

## con – dots (25) ⠒

Lower groupsign. Used only in the first syllable of a word. May be preceded by a hyphen or dash. Cannot be followed by a capital indicator/terminator.

## conceive – (con)cv

Shortform, stand-alone contraction. May be used as a proper name. May be followed by an *s* or an *'s*.

May be used as part of a longer word as long as the entire word is standing alone and if the longer word appears on the UEB Shortforms List.

## conceiving – (con)cvg

Shortform, stand-alone contraction. May be used as a proper name. May be followed by an *s* or an *'s*.

May be used as part of a longer word as long as the entire word is standing alone and if the longer word appears on the UEB Shortforms List.

## could – cd

Shortform, stand-alone contraction. May be used as a proper name. Use a grade 1 indicator if a letter sequence could be confused with a shortform (whole or part). May be followed by an *s* or an *'s*.

May be used as part of a longer word as long as the entire word is standing alone and if the longer word appears on the UEB Short-forms List.

## d – dots (145)

Must be preceded by a grade 1 indicator (letter sign) when representing a single letter.

## day – dots (5, 145)

Initial-letter contraction. Can be used as a groupsign or a wordsign.

### deceive – dcv

Shortform, stand-alone contraction. May be used as a proper name. Use a grade 1 indicator if a letter sequence could be confused with a shortform (whole or part). May be followed by an *s* or an *'s*.

May be used as part of a longer word as long as the entire word is standing alone and if the longer word appears on the UEB Short-forms List.

### deceiving – dcvg

Shortform, stand-alone contraction. May be used as a proper name. Use a grade 1 indicator if a letter sequence could be confused with a shortform (whole or part). May be followed by an *s* or an *'s*.

May be used as part of a longer word as long as the entire word is standing alone and if the longer word appears on the UEB Short-forms List.

### declare – dcl

Shortform, stand-alone contraction. May be used as a proper name. Use a grade 1 indicator if a letter sequence could be confused with a shortform (whole or part). May be followed by an *s* or an *'s*.

May be used as part of a longer word as long as the entire word is standing alone and if the longer word appears on the UEB Short-forms List.

## declaring – dclg

Shortform, stand-alone contraction. May be used as a proper name. Use a grade 1 indicator if a letter sequence could be confused with a shortform (whole or part). May be followed by an *s* or an *'s*.

May be used as part of a longer word as long as the entire word is standing alone and if the longer word appears on the UEB Short-forms List.

## dis – dots (256) ⠲

Lower groupsign. Used only in the first syllable of a word. May be preceded by a hyphen or dash. Cannot be followed by a capital indicator/terminator.

## do – d

Alphabetic wordsign, stand-alone, wordsign only. Can be used in contact with punctuation, including a hyphen. Can be used in contact with an apostrophe when the letters following are: *'d, 'll, 're, 's, 't,* or *'ve*.

## e – dots (15) ⠑

Must be preceded by a grade 1 indicator (letter sign) when representing a single letter.

## ea – dot 2 ⠂

Lower groupsign. Can be used only between letters or contractions within a word. Cannot be preceded or followed by a capital indicator/terminator. Cannot be divided between a prefix and root. All other one-cell contractions have precedence.

## ed – dots (1246) ⠫

Groupsign. Can be used in contact with punctuation, including a hyphen and an apostrophe. Can be used when separated by a prefix/suffix and a root. May be used to represent the name Ed or abbreviation *ed*. Cannot be used when separated by components of compound words.

## either – ei

Shortform, stand-alone contraction. May be used as a proper name. Use a grade 1 indicator if a letter sequence could be confused with a shortform (whole or part). May be followed by an s or an 's.

May be used as part of a longer word as long as the entire word is standing alone and if the longer word appears on the UEB Short-forms List.

## en – dots (26) ⠢

Lower groupsign. May be used when separated between syllables or a prefix and root. May not be used when separated between components of compound words. May not be used when standing alone.

## ence – dots (56, 15) ⠰⠑

Final-letter groupsign. Can be used only in the middle or at the end of a word. Must follow a letter, a contraction, a modified letter, or a ligatured letter. May directly follow a prefix. May not begin a new line in a divided word.

## enough – dots (26) ⠢

Lower wordsign. Can be used when the word it represents is standing alone. Can be used with an apostrophe. The capital indicator/terminator does not negate the stand-alone rule.

## er – dots (12456) ⠻

Groupsign. Can be used in contact with punctuation, including a hyphen and an apostrophe. Can be used when separated by a prefix/suffix and a root. May be used to represent the vocal sound of hesitation *er*. Cannot be used when separated by components of compound words.

## ever – dots (5, 15) ⠐⠑

Initial-letter contraction. Can be used when the stress is on the first *e* and when the letters are not preceded by *e* or *i*.

## every – e

Alphabetic wordsign, stand-alone, wordsign only. Can be used in contact with punctuation, including a hyphen. Can be used in contact with an apostrophe when the letters following are: *'d, 'll, 're, 's, 't,* or *'ve.*

## f – dots (124) ⠋

Must be preceded by a grade 1 indicator (letter sign) when representing a single letter.

## father – dots (5, 124) ⠐⠋

Initial-letter contraction. Can be used as a groupsign or a wordsign.

## ff – dots (235) ⠖

Lower groupsign. Can be used only between letters or contractions within a word. Cannot be preceded or followed by a capital indicator/terminator. All other one-cell contractions have precedence.

### first – f(st)

Shortform, stand-alone contraction. May be used as a proper name. Use a grade 1 indicator if a letter sequence could be confused with a shortform (whole or part). May be followed by an *s* or an *'s*.

May be used as part of a longer word. The longer word does not need to appear on the Shortforms List as long as the entire word is standing alone (including any affix with an apostrophe), the short-form begins the word, and it is not followed by a vowel or *y*.

### for – dots (123456) ⠿

Wordsign, strong contraction. Must be preceded and followed by a space within a sentence. May be preceded or followed by punctuation.

Groupsign. Can be used as a groupsign wherever the letters occur except where rules limit their use. Can be used when separated by a prefix/suffix and a root. Cannot be used when separated by components of compound words.

### friend – fr

Shortform, stand-alone contraction. May be used as a proper name. Use a grade 1 indicator if a letter sequence could be confused with a shortform (whole or part). May be followed by an *s* or an *'s*.

May be used as part of a longer word. The longer word does not need to appear on the Shortforms List as long as the entire word is standing alone (including any affix with an apostrophe), the short-form begins the word, and it is not followed by a vowel or *y*.

### from – f

Alphabetic wordsign, stand-alone, wordsign only. Can be used in contact with punctuation, including a hyphen. Can be used in contact with an apostrophe when the letters following are: *'d, 'll, 're, 's, 't,* or *'ve.*

## ful – dots (56, 123)

Final-letter groupsign. Can be used only in the middle or at the end of a word. Must follow a letter, a contraction, a modified letter, or a ligatured letter. May directly follow a prefix. May not begin a new line in a divided word.

## g – dots (1245)

Must be preceded by a grade 1 indicator (letter sign) when representing a single letter.

## gg – dots (2356)

Lower groupsign. Can be used only between letters or contractions within a word. Cannot be preceded or followed by a capital indicator/terminator. All other one-cell contractions have precedence.

## gh – dots (126)

Groupsign. Can be used in contact with punctuation, including a hyphen and an apostrophe. Can be used when separated by a prefix/suffix and a root. Cannot be used when separated by components of compound words.

## go – g

Alphabetic wordsign, stand-alone, wordsign only. Can be used in contact with punctuation, including a hyphen. Can be used in contact with an apostrophe when the letters following are: 'd, 'll, 're, 's, 't, or 've.

## good – gd

Shortform, stand-alone contraction. May be used as a proper name. Use a grade 1 indicator if a letter sequence could be confused with a shortform (whole or part). May be followed by an s or an 's.

May be used as part of a longer word. The longer word does not need to appear on the Shortforms List as long as the entire word is standing alone (including any affix with an apostrophe), the short-form begins the word, and it is not followed by a vowel or *y*.

### great – grt

Shortform, stand-alone contraction. May be used as a proper name. Use a grade 1 indicator if a letter sequence could be confused with a shortform (whole or part). May be followed by an *s* or an *'s*.

May be used as part of a longer word as long as the entire word is standing alone. The longer word does not need to appear on the Shortforms List as long as the entire word is standing alone (including any affix with an apostrophe).

### h – dots (125)

Must be preceded by a grade 1 indicator (letter sign) when representing a single letter.

### had – dots (456, 125)

Initial-letter contraction. Can be used as a groupsign or wordsign when it retains its original sound.

### have – h

Alphabetic wordsign, stand-alone, wordsign only. Can be used in contact with punctuation, including a hyphen. Can be used in contact with an apostrophe when the letters following are: *'d, 'll, 're, 's, 't,* or *'ve*.

### here – dots (5, 125)

Initial-letter contraction. Can be used as a groupsign or a wordsign when its letters are pronounced as a single syllable.

### herself – h(er)f

Shortform, stand-alone contraction. May be used as a proper name. May be followed by an *s* or an *'s*.

May be used as part of a longer word as long as the entire word is standing alone and if the longer word appears on the UEB Short-forms List.

### him – hm

Shortform, stand-alone contraction. May be used as a proper name. Use a grade 1 indicator if a letter sequence could be confused with a shortform (whole or part).

May be used as part of a longer word as long as the entire word is standing alone and if the longer word appears on the UEB Short-forms List.

### himself – hmf

Shortform, stand-alone contraction. May be used as a proper name. Use a grade 1 indicator if a letter sequence could be confused with a shortform (whole or part). May be followed by an s or an 's.

May be used as part of a longer word as long as the entire word is standing alone and if the longer word appears on the UEB Short-forms List.

### his – dots (236) ⠦

Lower wordsign. Can be used when the word it represents is standing alone. Cannot be used when in contact with any punctuation sign, including the hyphen and dash, which has only lower dots. The capital indicator/terminator does not negate this rule.

### i – dots (24) ⠊

Letter, wordsign (when capitalized), stand-alone.

### immediate – imm

Shortform, stand-alone contraction. May be used as a proper name. Use a grade 1 indicator if a letter sequence could be confused with a shortform (whole or part). May be followed by an s or an 's.

May be used as part of a longer word as long as the entire word is standing alone and if the longer word appears on the UEB Short-forms List.

## in – dots (35) ⠊⠒

Lower wordsign. May be used whenever it occurs as long as it or the sequence of cells adjacent contains an upper dot. All quotes are considered lower cell.

Lower groupsign. May be used when separated between syllables or a prefix and root. May not be used when separated between components of compound words.

## ing – dots (346) ⠭

Groupsign. Can be used in contact with punctuation, including a hyphen and an apostrophe. Can be used when separated by a prefix/suffix and a root. Cannot be used when separated by components of compound words. Cannot be used at the beginning of a word.

## it – x

Alphabetic wordsign, stand-alone, wordsign only. Can be used in contact with punctuation, including a hyphen. Can be used in contact with an apostrophe when the letters following are: 'd, 'll, 're, 's, 't, or 've.

## its – xs

Shortform, stand-alone contraction. May be used as a proper name. Use a grade 1 indicator if a letter sequence could be confused with a shortform (whole or part). May be followed by an s or an 's.

May be used as part of a longer word as long as the entire word is standing alone and if the longer word appears on the UEB Short-forms List.

## itself – xf

Shortform, stand-alone contraction. May be used as a proper name. Use a grade 1 indicator if a letter sequence could be confused with a shortform (whole or part). May be followed by an *s* or an *'s*.

May be used as part of a longer word as long as the entire word is standing alone and if the longer word appears on the UEB Shortforms List.

## ity – dots (56, 13456)

Final-letter groupsign. Can be used only in the middle or at the end of a word. Must follow a letter, a contraction, a modified letter, or a ligatured letter. May directly follow a prefix. May not begin a new line in a divided word. Cannot use in *biscuity, dacoity, fruity, hoity-toity,* and *rabbit.*

## j – dots (245)

Must be preceded by a grade 1 indicator (letter sign) when representing a single letter.

## just – j

Alphabetic wordsign, stand-alone, wordsign only. Can be used in contact with punctuation, including a hyphen. Can be used in contact with an apostrophe when the letters following are: *'d, 'll, 're, 's, 't,* or *'ve.*

## k – dots (13)

Must be preceded by a grade 1 indicator (letter sign) when representing a single letter.

## know – dots (5, 13)

Initial-letter contraction. Can be used as a groupsign or a wordsign.

## knowledge – k

Alphabetic wordsign, stand-alone, wordsign only. Can be used in contact with punctuation, including a hyphen. Can be used in contact with an apostrophe when the letters following are: *'d, 'll, 're, 's, 't,* or *'ve.*

## l – dots (123)

Must be preceded by a grade 1 indicator (letter sign) when representing a single letter.

## less – dots (46, 234)

Final-letter groupsign. Can be used only in the middle or at the end of a word. Must follow a letter, a contraction, a modified letter, or a ligatured letter. May directly follow a prefix. May not begin a new line in a divided word.

## letter – lr

Shortform, stand-alone contraction. May be used as a proper name. Use a grade 1 indicator if a letter sequence could be confused with a shortform (whole or part). May be followed by an s or an *'s*.

May be used as part of a longer word. The longer word does not need to appear on the Shortforms List as long as the entire word is standing alone (including any affix with an apostrophe), the shortform begins the word, and it is not followed by a vowel or *y*.

## like – l

Alphabetic wordsign, stand-alone, wordsign only. Can be used in contact with punctuation, including a hyphen. Can be used in contact with an apostrophe when the letters following are: *'d, 'll, 're, 's, 't,* or *'ve.*

### little – ll

Shortform, stand-alone contraction. May be used as a proper name. Use a grade 1 indicator if a letter sequence could be confused with a shortform (whole or part). May be followed by an *s* or an *'s*.

May be used as part of a longer word. The longer word does not need to appear on the Shortforms List as long as the entire word is standing alone (including any affix with an apostrophe), the short-form begins the word, and it is not followed by a vowel or *y*.

### lord – dots (5, 123)

Initial-letter contraction. Can be used as a groupsign or a wordsign.

### m – dots (134)

Must be preceded by a grade 1 indicator (letter sign) when representing a single letter.

### many – dots (456, 134)

Initial-letter contraction. Can be used as a groupsign or a wordsign.

### ment – dots (56, 2345)

Final-letter groupsign. Can be used only in the middle or at the end of a word. Must follow a letter, a contraction, a modified letter, or a ligatured letter. May directly follow a prefix. May not begin a new line in a divided word.

### more – m

Alphabetic wordsign, stand-alone, wordsign only. Can be used in contact with punctuation, including a hyphen. Can be used in contact with an apostrophe when the letters following are: *'d, 'll, 're, 's, 't,* or *'ve.*

### mother – dots (5, 134)

Initial-letter contraction. Can be used as a groupsign or a wordsign.

## much – m(ch)

Shortform, stand-alone contraction. May be used as a proper name. May be followed by an *s* or an *'s*.

May be used as part of a longer word as long as the entire word is standing alone and if the longer word appears on the UEB Short-forms List.

## must – m(st)

Shortform, stand-alone contraction. May be used as a proper name. May be followed by an *s* or an *'s*.

May be used as part of a longer word as long as the entire word is standing alone and if the longer word appears on the UEB Short-forms List.

## myself – myf

Shortform, stand-alone contraction. May be used as a proper name. Use a grade 1 indicator if a letter sequence could be confused with a shortform (whole or part). May be followed by an *s* or an *'s*.

May be used as part of a longer word as long as the entire word is standing alone and if the longer word appears on the UEB Short-forms List.

## n – dots (1345)

Must be preceded by a grade 1 indicator (letter sign) when representing a single letter.

## name – dots (5, 1345)

Initial-letter contraction. Can be used as a groupsign or a wordsign when its letters are pronounced as a single syllable.

## necessary – nec

Shortform, stand-alone contraction. May be used as a proper name. Use a grade 1 indicator if a letter sequence could be confused with a shortform (whole or part). May be followed by an *s* or an *'s*.

May be used as part of a longer word as long as the entire word is standing alone and if the longer word appears on the UEB Short-forms List.

## neither – nei

Shortform, stand-alone contraction. May be used as a proper name. Use a grade 1 indicator if a letter sequence could be confused with a shortform (whole or part). May be followed by an *s* or an *'s*.

May be used as part of a longer word as long as the entire word is standing alone and if the longer word appears on the UEB Short-forms List.

## ness – dots (56, 234)

Final-letter groupsign. Can be used only in the middle or at the end of a word. Must follow a letter, a contraction, a modified letter, or a ligatured letter. May directly follow a prefix. May not begin a new line in a divided word. Cannot be used when the feminine ending *ess* is added to a word ending in *en* or *in*.

## not – n

Alphabetic wordsign, stand-alone, wordsign only. Can be used in contact with punctuation, including a hyphen. Can be used in contact with an apostrophe when the letters following are: *'d, 'll, 're, 's, 't,* or *'ve*.

## o – dots (135)

Letter, wordsign, stand-alone.

## of – dots (12356) ⠷

Wordsign, strong contraction. Must be preceded and followed by a space within a sentence. May be preceded or followed by punctuation.

Groupsign. Can be used as a groupsign wherever the letters occur except where rules limit their use. Can be used when separated by a prefix/suffix and a root. Cannot be used when separated by components of compound words.

## one – dots (5, 135) ⠨ ⠕

Initial-letter contraction. Can be used as a groupsign or wordsign when the letters are pronounced as one syllable. Exceptions: *honest*, *monetary* (and their derivatives), and words ending in *oney*. Cannot be used when preceded by the letter *o*.

## oneself – (one)f

Shortform, stand-alone contraction. May be used as a proper name. May be followed by an *s* or an *'s*.

May be used as part of a longer word as long as the entire word is standing alone and if the longer word appears on the UEB Shortforms List.

## ong – dots (56, 1245) ⠰ ⠛

Final-letter groupsign. Can be used only in the middle or at the end of a word. Must follow a letter, a contraction, a modified letter, or a ligatured letter. May directly follow a prefix. May not begin a new line in a divided word.

## ou – dots (1256) ⠹

Groupsign. Can be used in contact with punctuation, including a hyphen and an apostrophe. Can be used when separated by a prefix/suffix and a root. Cannot be used when separated by components of compound words.

**ought – dots (5, 1256)** ⠨⠡

Initial-letter contraction. Wordsign or groupsign.

**ound – dots (46, 145)** ⠨⠙

Final-letter groupsign. Can be used only in the middle or at the end of a word. Must follow a letter, a contraction, a modified letter, or a ligatured letter. May directly follow a prefix. May not begin a new line in a divided word.

**ount – dots (46, 2345)** ⠨⠞

Final-letter groupsign. Can be used only in the middle or at the end of a word. Must follow a letter, a contraction, a modified letter, or a ligatured letter. May directly follow a prefix. May not begin a new line in a divided word.

**ourselves – (ou)rvs**

Shortform, stand-alone contraction. May be used as a proper name. May be followed by an *s* or an *'s*.

May be used as part of a longer word as long as the entire word is standing alone and if the longer word appears on the UEB Short-forms List.

**out – (ou)**

Wordsign, stand-alone. Can be used in contact with punctuation and composition signs. Can be used in contact with an apostrophe when the letters following are: *'d, 'll, 're, 's, 't,* or *'ve*.

**ow – dots (246)** ⠪

Wordsign. May be used to represent the exclamation *"Ow!"*

Groupsign. Can be used in contact with punctuation, including a hyphen and an apostrophe. Can be used when separated by a prefix/suffix and a root. Cannot be used when separated by components of compound words.

## p – dots (1234)

Must be preceded by a grade 1 indicator (letter sign) when representing a single letter.

## paid – pd

Shortform, stand-alone contraction. May be used as a proper name. Use a grade 1 indicator if a letter sequence could be confused with a shortform (whole or part). May be followed by an s or an 's.

May be used as part of a longer word as long as the entire word is standing alone and if the longer word appears on the UEB Short-forms List.

## part – dots (5, 1234)

Initial-letter contraction. Can be used as a groupsign or a wordsign.

## people – p

Alphabetic wordsign, stand-alone, wordsign only. Can be used in contact with punctuation, including a hyphen. Can be used in contact with an apostrophe when the letters following are: 'd, 'll, 're, 's, 't, or 've.

## perceive – p(er)cv

Shortform, stand-alone contraction. May be used as a proper name. May be followed by an s or an 's.

May be used as part of a longer word as long as the entire word is standing alone and if the longer word appears on the UEB Short-forms List.

## perceiving – p(er)cvg

Shortform, stand-alone contraction. May be used as a proper name. May be followed by an s or an 's.

May be used as part of a longer word as long as the entire word is standing alone and if the longer word appears on the UEB Short-forms List.

### perhaps – p(er)h

Shortform, stand-alone contraction. May be used as a proper name. May be followed by an *s* or an *'s.*

May be used as part of a longer word as long as the entire word is standing alone and if the longer word appears on the UEB Short-forms List.

### q – dots (12345)

Must be preceded by a grade 1 indicator (letter sign) when repre-senting a single letter.

### question – dots (5, 12345)

Initial-letter contraction. Can be used as a groupsign or a wordsign.

### quick – qk

Shortform, stand-alone contraction. May be used as a proper name. Use a grade 1 indicator if a letter sequence could be confused with a shortform (whole or part). May be followed by an *s* or an *'s.*

May be used as part of a longer word. The longer word does not need to appear on the Shortforms List as long as the entire word is standing alone (including any affix with an apostrophe), the short-form begins the word, and it is not followed by a vowel or *y.*

### quite – q

Alphabetic wordsign, stand-alone, wordsign only. Can be used in contact with punctuation, including a hyphen. Can be used in con-tact with an apostrophe when the letters following are: *'d, 'll, 're, 's, 't,* or *'ve.*

## r – dots (1235) ⠗

Must be preceded by a grade 1 indicator (letter sign) when representing a single letter.

## rather – r

Alphabetic wordsign, stand-alone, wordsign only. Can be used in contact with punctuation, including a hyphen. Can be used in contact with an apostrophe when the letters following are: 'd, 'll, 're, 's, 't, or 've.

## receive – rcv

Shortform, stand-alone contraction. May be used as a proper name. Use a grade 1 indicator if a letter sequence could be confused with a shortform (whole or part). May be followed by an s or an 's.

May be used as part of a longer word as long as the entire word is standing alone and if the longer word appears on the UEB Shortforms List.

## receiving – rcvg

Shortform, stand-alone contraction. May be used as a proper name. Use a grade 1 indicator if a letter sequence could be confused with a shortform (whole or part). May be followed by an s or an 's.

May be used as part of a longer word as long as the entire word is standing alone and if the longer word appears on the UEB Shortforms List.

## rejoice – rjc

Shortform, stand-alone contraction. May be used as a proper name. Use a grade 1 indicator if a letter sequence could be confused with a shortform (whole or part). May be followed by an s or an 's.

May be used as part of a longer word as long as the entire word is standing alone and if the longer word appears on the UEB Shortforms List.

## rejoicing – rjcg

Shortform, stand-alone contraction. May be used as a proper name. Use a grade 1 indicator if a letter sequence could be confused with a shortform (whole or part). May be followed by an *s* or an *'s*.

May be used as part of a longer word as long as the entire word is standing alone and if the longer word appears on the UEB Short-forms List.

## right – dots (5, 1235)

Initial-letter contraction. Can be used as a groupsign or a wordsign.

## s – dots (234)

Must be preceded by a grade 1 indicator (letter sign) when representing a single letter.

## said – sd

Shortform, stand-alone contraction. May be used as a proper name. Use a grade 1 indicator if a letter sequence could be confused with a shortform (whole or part). May be followed by an *s* or an *'s*.

May be used as part of a longer word as long as the entire word is standing alone and if the longer word appears on the UEB Short-forms List.

## sh – dots (146)

Groupsign. Can be used in contact with punctuation, including a hyphen and an apostrophe. Can be used when separated by a prefix/suffix and a root. Cannot be used when the *s* and the *h* are pronounced separately. Cannot be used when separated by components of compound words.

## shall – (sh)

Wordsign, stand-alone. Can be used in contact with punctuation and composition signs. Can be used in contact with an apostrophe when the letters following are: 'd, 'll, 're, 's, 't, or 've.

## should – (sh)d

Shortform, stand-alone contraction. May be used as a proper name. Use a grade 1 indicator if a letter sequence could be confused with a shortform (whole or part). May be followed by an s or an 's.

May be used as part of a longer word as long as the entire word is standing alone and if the longer word appears on the UEB Short-forms List.

## sion – dots (46, 1345)

Final-letter groupsign. Can be used only in the middle or at the end of a word. Must follow a letter, a contraction, a modified letter, or a ligatured letter. May directly follow a prefix. May not begin a new line in a divided word.

## so – s

Alphabetic wordsign, stand-alone, wordsign only. Can be used in contact with punctuation, including a hyphen. Can be used in contact with an apostrophe when the letters following are: 'd, 'll, 're, 's, 't, or 've.

## some – dots (5, 234)

Initial-letter contraction. Can be used as a groupsign or wordsign when the letters form a syllable of the root word.

## spirit – dots (456, 234)

Initial-letter contraction. Can be used as a groupsign or a wordsign.

## st – dots (34) ⠌

Groupsign. Can be used in contact with punctuation, including a hyphen and an apostrophe. Can be used when separated by a prefix/suffix and a root. Cannot be used when separated by components of compound words.

## still – (st)

Wordsign, stand-alone. Can be used in contact with punctuation and composition signs. Can be used in contact with an apostrophe when the letters following are: 'd, 'll, 're, 's, 't, or 've.

## such – s(ch)

Shortform, stand-alone contraction. May be used as a proper name. May be followed by an s or an 's.

May be used as part of a longer word as long as the entire word is standing alone and if the longer word appears on the UEB Short-forms List.

## t – dots (2345) ⠞

Must be preceded by a grade 1 indicator (letter sign) when representing a single letter.

## th – dots (1456) ⠹

Groupsign. Can be used in contact with punctuation, including a hyphen and an apostrophe. Can be used when separated by a prefix/suffix and a root. Cannot be used when separated by components of compound words. Cannot be used when the t and the h are pronounced separately.

## that – t

Alphabetic wordsign, stand-alone, wordsign only. Can be used in contact with punctuation, including a hyphen. Can be used in contact with an apostrophe when the letters following are: 'd, 'll, 're, 's, 't, or 've.

## the – dots (2346)

Wordsign, strong contraction. Must be preceded and followed by a space within a sentence. May be preceded or followed by punctuation.

Groupsign. Can be used as a groupsign wherever the letters occur except where rules limit their use. Can be used when separated by a prefix/suffix and a root. Cannot be used when separated by components of compound words.

## their – dots (456, 2346)

Initial-letter contraction. Can be used as a groupsign or a wordsign.

## themselves – (the)mvs

Shortform, stand-alone contraction. May be used as a proper name. May be followed by an s or an 's.

May be used as part of a longer word as long as the entire word is standing alone and if the longer word appears on the UEB Shortforms List.

## there – dots (5, 2346)

Initial-letter contraction. Wordsign or groupsign. May be used when its meaning as a whole word is retained.

## these – dots (45, 2346)

Initial-letter contraction. Wordsign or groupsign. May be used when its meaning as a whole word is retained.

## this – (th)

Wordsign, stand-alone. Can be used in contact with punctuation and composition signs. Can be used in contact with an apostrophe when the letters following are: 'd, 'll, 're, 's, 't, or 've.

**those – dots (45, 1456)** ⠳ ⠮

Initial-letter contraction. Wordsign or groupsign. May be used when its meaning as a whole word is retained.

**through – dots (5, 1456)** ⠐ ⠮

Initial-letter contraction. Can be used as a groupsign or a wordsign.

**thyself – (th)yf**

Shortform, stand-alone contraction. May be used as a proper name. May be followed by an s or an 's.

May be used as part of a longer word as long as the entire word is standing alone and if the longer word appears on the UEB Short-forms List.

**time – dots (5, 2345)** ⠐ ⠞

Initial-letter contraction. Can be used as a groupsign or wordsign when it retains its original sound.

**tion – dots (56, 1345)** ⠰ ⠝

Final-letter groupsign. Can be used only in the middle or at the end of a word. Must follow a letter, a contraction, a modified letter, or a ligatured letter. May directly follow a prefix. May not begin a new line in a divided word.

**today – td**

Shortform, stand-alone contraction. May be used as a proper name. Use a grade 1 indicator if a letter sequence could be confused with a shortform (whole or part). May be followed by an s or an 's.

May be used as part of a longer word as long as the entire word is standing alone and if the longer word appears on the UEB Short-forms List.

### together – tgr

Shortform, stand-alone contraction. May be used as a proper name. Use a grade 1 indicator if a letter sequence could be confused with a shortform (whole or part). May be followed by an s or an 's.

May be used as part of a longer word as long as the entire word is standing alone and if the longer word appears on the UEB Short-forms List.

### tomorrow – tm

Shortform, stand-alone contraction. May be used as a proper name. Use a grade 1 indicator if a letter sequence could be confused with a shortform (whole or part). May be followed by an s or an 's.

May be used as part of a longer word as long as the entire word is standing alone and if the longer word appears on the UEB Short-forms List.

### tonight – tn

Shortform, stand-alone contraction. May be used as a proper name. Use a grade 1 indicator if a letter sequence could be confused with a shortform (whole or part). May be followed by an s or an 's.

May be used as part of a longer word as long as the entire word is standing alone and if the longer word appears on the UEB Short-forms List.

### u – dots (136)

Must be preceded by a grade 1 indicator (letter sign) when representing a single letter.

### under – dots (5, 136)

Initial-letter contraction. Can be used as a groupsign or wordsign. Cannot be used when preceded by the vowels *a* or *o* or when the letters *un* form a prefix.

**upon – dots (45, 136)** ⠠⠩

Initial-letter contraction. Wordsign or groupsign. May be used when its meaning as a whole word is retained.

**us – u**

Alphabetic wordsign, stand-alone, wordsign only. Can be used in contact with punctuation, including a hyphen. Can be used in contact with an apostrophe when the letters following are: *'d, 'll, 're, 's, 't,* or *'ve.*

**v – dots (1236)** ⠧

Must be preceded by a grade 1 indicator (letter sign) when representing a single letter.

**very – v**

Alphabetic wordsign, stand-alone, wordsign only. Can be used in contact with punctuation, including a hyphen. Can be used in contact with an apostrophe when the letters following are: *'d, 'll, 're, 's, 't,* or *'ve.*

**w – dots (2456)** ⠺

Must be preceded by a grade 1 indicator (letter sign) when representing a single letter.

**was – dots (356)** ⠴

Lower wordsign. Can be used when the word it represents is standing alone. Cannot be used when in contact with any punctuation sign, including the hyphen and dash, which has only lower dots. The capital indicator/terminator does not negate this rule.

## were – dots (2356) ⠶

Lower wordsign. Can be used when the word it represents is standing alone. Cannot be used when in contact with any punctuation sign, including the hyphen and dash, which has only lower dots. The capital indicator/terminator does not negate this rule.

## wh – dots (156) ⠱

Groupsign. Can be used in contact with punctuation, including a hyphen and an apostrophe. Can be used when separated by a prefix/suffix and a root. Cannot be used when separated by components of compound words. Cannot be used when the *w* and the *h* are pronounced separately.

## where – dots (5, 156) ⠐⠱

Initial-letter contraction. Can be used as a groupsign or a wordsign.

## which – (wh)

Wordsign, stand-alone. Can be used in contact with punctuation and composition signs. Can be used in contact with an apostrophe when the letters following are: *'d, 'll, 're, 's, 't,* or *'ve.*

## whose – dots (45, 156) ⠘⠱

Initial-letter contraction. Wordsign or groupsign. May be used when its meaning as a whole word is retained.

## will – w

Alphabetic wordsign, stand-alone, wordsign only. Can be used in contact with punctuation, including a hyphen. Can be used in contact with an apostrophe when the letters following are: *'d, 'll, 're, 's, 't,* or *'ve.*

## with – dots (23456) ⠿

Wordsign, strong contraction. Must be preceded and followed by a space within a sentence. May be preceded or followed by punctuation.

Groupsign. Can be used as a groupsign wherever the letters occur except where rules limit their use. Can be used when separated by a prefix/suffix and a root. Cannot be used when separated by components of compound words.

## word – dots (45, 2456) ⠨⠺

Initial-letter contraction. Can be used as a groupsign or a wordsign.

## work – dots (5, 2456) ⠐⠺

Initial-letter contraction. Can be used as a groupsign or a wordsign.

## world – dots (456, 2456) ⠸⠺

Initial-letter contraction. Can be used as a groupsign or a wordsign.

## would – wd

Shortform, stand-alone contraction. May be used as a proper name. Use a grade 1 indicator if a letter sequence could be confused with a shortform (whole or part). May be followed by an *s* or an *'s*.

May be used as part of a longer word as long as the entire word is standing alone and if the longer word appears on the UEB Shortforms List.

## x – dots (1346) ⠭

Must be preceded by a grade 1 indicator (letter sign) when representing a single letter.

## y – dots (13456)

Must be preceded by a grade 1 indicator (letter sign) when representing a single letter.

## you – y

Alphabetic wordsign, stand-alone, wordsign only. Can be used in contact with punctuation, including a hyphen. Can be used in contact with an apostrophe when the letters following are: 'd, 'll, 're, 's, 't, or 've.

## young – dots (5, 13456)

Initial-letter contraction. Can be used as a groupsign or a wordsign.

## your – yr

Shortform, stand-alone contraction. May be used as a proper name. Use a grade 1 indicator if a letter sequence could be confused with a shortform (whole or part). May be followed by an s or an 's.

May be used as part of a longer word as long as the entire word is standing alone and if the longer word appears on the UEB Short-forms List.

## yourself – yrf

Shortform, stand-alone contraction. May be used as a proper name. Use a grade 1 indicator if a letter sequence could be confused with a shortform (whole or part). May be followed by an s or an 's.

May be used as part of a longer word as long as the entire word is standing alone and if the longer word appears on the UEB Short-forms List.

## yourselves – yrvs

Shortform, stand-alone contraction. May be used as a proper name. Use a grade 1 indicator if a letter sequence could be confused with a shortform (whole or part). May be followed by an *s* or an *'s*.

May be used as part of a longer word as long as the entire word is standing alone and if the longer word appears on the UEB Short-forms List.

## z – dots (1356) ⠵

Must be preceded by a grade 1 indicator (letter sign) when repre-senting a single letter.

# APPENDIX
# Shortforms List

This Appendix provides the Shortforms List from *The Rules of Unified English Braille*.* The Shortforms List is maintained by the International Council on English Braille Code Maintenance Committee. Refer to Section 10.9, Contractions, for the rules on the use of shortforms.

## THE LIST

Added "s" and apostrophe "s"

When an "s" or apostrophe "s" is added to any word on the list, use the shortform with the following three exceptions:

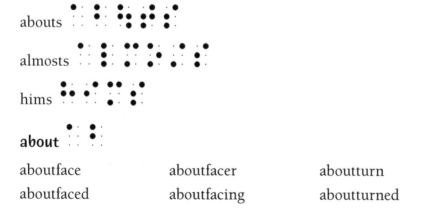

abouts

almosts

hims

**about**

| aboutface | aboutfacer | aboutturn |
| aboutfaced | aboutfacing | aboutturned |

---

* Reprinted with permission of the International Council on English Braille from Simpson, C. (Ed.). (2013). Appendix 1: Shortforms list. In *The Rules of Unified English Braille* (2nd ed.). Lindisfarne, Australia: Round Table on Information Access for People with Print Disabilities Inc. and International Council on English Braille. Retrieved from http://www.iceb.org/ueb.html

eastabout

gadabout

hereabout

knockabout

layabout

northabout

rightabout

roundabout

roustabout

runabout

southabout

stirabout

thereabout

turnabout

walkabout

westabout

whereabout

**above**

aboveboard

aboveground

abovementioned

hereinabove

**according**

accordingly                unaccording                unaccordingly

**across**

readacross

**after**

afterbattle

afterbirth

afterbreakfast

afterburn

afterburned

afterburner

afterburning

aftercare

afterclap

aftercoffee

afterdamp

afterdark

afterdeck

afterdinner

afterflow

aftergame

afterglow

afterguard

afterhatch

afterhatches

afterhour

afterlife

afterlight

afterlives

afterlunch

afterlunches

aftermarket

aftermatch

aftermatches

aftermath

aftermeeting

aftermidday

aftermidnight

aftermost

afterpain

afterparties

afterparty

afterpiece

afterplay

aftersale

afterschool

aftersensation

aftershave

aftershock

aftershow

aftershower

aftersupper

aftertaste

aftertax

aftertaxes

aftertea

aftertheatre

afterthought

aftertime

aftertreatment

afterword

afterwork

afterworld

hereafter

hereinafter

morningafter

thereafter

thereinafter

whereafter

whereinafter

**afternoon**

afternoontea            goodafternoon            midafternoon

**afterward**

**again**

hereagain              thereagain              whereagain

hereinagain            thereinagain            whereinagain

**against**

hereagainst            thereagainst            whereagainst

**almost**

**already**

**also**

**although**

**altogether**

**always** ⠿

**because** ⠿

**before** ⠿
beforehand

**behind** ⠿
behindhand

**below** ⠿

| | | |
|---|---|---|
| belowdeck | belowground | belowmentioned |

**beneath** ⠿
| | |
|---|---|
| beneathdeck | beneathground |

**beside** ⠿

**between** ⠿
| | | |
|---|---|---|
| betweendeck | betweentime | betweenwhile |

**beyond** ⠿

**blind** ⠿

| | | |
|---|---|---|
| blindfish | blindly | blindsided |
| blindfishes | blindman | blindsider |
| blindfold | blindmen | blindsiding |
| blindfolded | blindness | blindsight |
| blindfolder | blindnesses | blindstories |
| blindfolding | blindside | blindstory |

| | | |
|---|---|---|
| blindworm | deafblind | snowblind |
| colorblind | deafblindness | snowblindness |
| colorblindness | deafblindnesses | snowblindnesses |
| colorblindnesses | purblind | unblindfold |
| colourblind | purblindly | unblindfolded |
| colourblindness | purblindness | unblindfolding |
| colourblindnesses | purblindnesses | |

**braille** ⠿ [See also Section 10.9.3 (a)]

| | | |
|---|---|---|
| brailled | braille | rebrailled |
| brailler | misbraille | rebrailler |
| braillewriter | misbrailled | unbraille |
| braillewriting | rebraille | unbrailled |

**children** ⠿ [See also Section 10.9.3 (b)]

| | | |
|---|---|---|
| children'swear | godchildren | lovechildren |
| brainchildren | grandchildren | schoolchildren |
| fosterchildren | greatgrandchildren | stepchildren |

**conceive** ⠿

| | |
|---|---|
| conceived | conceiver |

**conceiving** ⠿

**could** ⠿

| | | |
|---|---|---|
| could've | couldest | couldn't've |
| coulda | couldn't | couldst |

**deceive** ⠿

| | | |
|---|---|---|
| deceived | archdeceiver | undeceived |
| deceiver | undeceive | undeceiver |

**deceiving**

undeceiving

**declare**

| declared | undeclare |
|----------|-----------|
| declarer | undeclared |

**declaring**

**either**

**first** [See also Section 10.9.3 (c)]

| firstaid | firstfruiting | firstnighter |
|----------|---------------|--------------|
| firstaider | firstgeneration | firstrate |
| firstborn | firsthand | firstrated |
| firstclass | firsthanded | firstrating |
| firstclasses | firstling | firststring |
| firstday | firstly | feetfirst |
| firstdayer | firstness | headfirst |
| firstfruit | firstnight | tailfirst |

**friend** [See also Section 10.9.3 (c)]

| friendless | friendly | girlfriend |
|------------|----------|------------|
| friendlessness | friendship | guyfriend |
| friendlessnesses | befriend | ladyfriend |
| friendlier | boyfriend | manfriend |
| friendlies | defriend | menfriends |
| friendliest | galfriend | penfriend |
| friendliness | gentlemanfriend | schoolfriend |
| friendlinesses | gentlemenfriends | unfriend |

unfriendlier

unfriendliest

unfriendliness

unfriendlinesses

unfriendly

womanfriend

womenfriends

## good ⠿⠿ [See also Section 10.9.3 (c)]

goodafternoon

goodby

goodbye

goodbyeing

goodbying

goodday

gooder

goodest

goodevening

goodfellow

goodfellowship

goodhearted

goodheartedly

goodheartedness

goodhumor

goodhumored

goodhumoredly

goodhumoredness

goodhumorednesses

goodhumour

goodhumoured

goodhumouredly

goodhumouredness

goodhumoured-
nesses

goodie

goodish

goodlier

goodliest

goodliness

goodlook

goodlooker

goodlooking

goodly

goodman

goodmen

goodmorning

goodnature

goodnatured

goodnaturedly

good-naturedness

goodness

goodnesses

goodnight

goodsize

goodsized

goodtempered

goodtemperedly

goodtime

goodun

goodwife

goodwill

goodwilled

goodwives

goody

goodyear

feelgood

scattergood

supergood

## great ⠿⠿⠿ [See also Section 10.9.3 (a)]

greataunt

greatbatch

greatcircle

greatcoat

greaten

greatened

greatener

greatening

greater

greatest

greatgrandaunt

greatgrandchild

greatgrandchildren

greatgranddad

greatgranddaughter

greatgrandfather

greatgrandfather-
hood

greatgrandma

greatgrandmother

greatgrandmother-
hood

greatgrandnephew

greatgrandniece

greatgrandpa

greatgrandparent

greatgrandparent-
hood

greatgrandson

greatgranduncle

greathearted

greatheartedly

greatheartedness

greatheartednesses

greatly

greatnephew

greatness

greatnesses

greatniece

greatsword

greatuncle

**herself** ⠿

**him** ⠿

himbo                himboes

**himself** ⠿

**immediate** ⠿

immediately          immediateness

**its** ⠿

**itself** ⠿

**letter** ⠿ [See also Section 10.9.3 (c)]

letterbomb

letterbombed

letterbomber

letterbombing

letterbox

letterboxed

letterboxer

letterboxes

letterboxing

letterbodies

letterbody

lettered

letterer

letterform

letterhead

| letterheading | letterpresses | chainletter |
| letterling | letterpressing | hateletter |
| letterman | letterquality | loveletter |
| lettermen | letterspace | newsletter |
| letteropener | letterspaced | reletter |
| letterperfect | letterspacing | relettered |
| letterpress | lettertext | relettering |
| letterpressed | bloodletter | unlettered |

**little** [See also Section 10.9.3 (c)]

| littled | littler | belittlement |
| littleneck | littlest | belittler |
| littleness | belittle | |
| littlenesses | belittled | |

**much**

| muchly | forasmuch | insomuch |
| muchness | inasmuch | overmuch |

**must**

| must've | mustiest | mustn't've |
| musta | mustily | musty |
| mustard | mustiness | |
| mustier | mustn't | |

**myself**

**necessary**

unnecessary

**neither**

oneself

ourselves

paid

| highlypaid | poorlypaid | underpaid |
| illpaid | postpaid | unpaid |
| lowlypaid | prepaid | wellpaid |
| overpaid | repaid | |

perceive

| perceived | apperceived | misperceived |
| perceiver | apperceiver | misperceiver |
| apperceive | misperceive | unperceived |

perceiving

| apperceiving | misperceiving | unperceiving |

perhaps

perhapses

quick     [See also Section 10.9.3 (c)]

| quickdraw | quickfiring | quicklime |
| quicken | quickfreeze | quickly |
| quickened | quickfreezing | quickness |
| quickener | quickfroze | quicknesses |
| quickening | quickfrozen | quicksand |
| quicker | quickie | quickset |
| quickest | quickish | quicksilver |
| quickfire | quickishly | quicksilvered |

| | | |
|---|---|---|
| quicksilvering | quickstepping | quick-wittedness |
| quicksnap | quicktempered | quicky |
| quickstep | quicktime | doublequick |
| quickstepped | quick-witted | superquick |
| quickstepper | quickwittedly | unquick |

**receive**

| | | |
|---|---|---|
| received | receivership | preceiver |
| receiver | preceive | unreceived |

**receiving**

preceiving

**rejoice**

| | | |
|---|---|---|
| rejoiced | rejoicer | unrejoiceful |
| rejoiceful | unrejoice | unrejoicefully |
| rejoicefully | unrejoiced | unrejoicefulness |
| rejoicefulness | unrejoicer | |

**rejoicing**

| | | |
|---|---|---|
| rejoicingly | unrejoicing | unrejoicingly |

**said**

| | | |
|---|---|---|
| saidest | aforesaid | gainsaid |
| saidst | foresaid | missaid |

**should**

| | | |
|---|---|---|
| should've | shouldest | shouldn't've |
| shoulda | shouldn't | shouldst |

such ⠩

suchlike                  nonsuch
nonesuch                  somesuch

themselves ⠒⠢⠮⠧⠎

thyself ⠹⠽⠋

today ⠞⠙

together ⠞⠛⠗

togetherness

tomorrow ⠞⠍

tonight ⠞⠝

would ⠺⠙

would've            wouldn't've            'twoulda
woulda              wouldst                'twouldn't
wouldest            'twould                'twouldn't've
wouldn't            'twould've

your ⠽⠗

yourself ⠽⠗⠋

do-it-yourselfer

yourselves ⠽⠗⠧⠎

Mary F. Burns, MSEd, is an itinerant teacher of students who are visually impaired and a certified orientation and mobility specialist, serving in school districts throughout Texas, Wisconsin, and Illinois. She is the author of the first edition of *The Burns Braille Transcription Dictionary*, published in 1991. She developed, organized, and led the first Wisconsin Vision Teachers conference in 1993 and again in 1996 and served on the board of the Wisconsin chapter of the Association for Education and Rehabilitation of the Blind and Visually Impaired. She has been a braille transcriber and certified teacher of braille for over 30 years.

Lightning Source UK Ltd.
Milton Keynes UK
UKOW05f0630170417

299265UK00016B/622/P